My Alphabet is Super! (Normies)

Book 5 of the Series: My Alphabet Is...

Text and Illustrations
@Copyright David Taylor II 2019
All Rights Reserved.

1st Edition, Softcover
Published in 2019 by
HODT Books, PO Box 693
Skokie, IL 60076-0693
ISBN 978-1-7336248-5-5
www.HODTBooks.com

All rights reserved. No part of this book may be reproduced or transmitted in any form, or by any means, electronic, mechanical, digital, photocopying, recording, or by any storage and retrieval information system, or any technology created in the future relative to the publishing date of this book, without the express written permission of the publisher.

This book is a work of fiction. Names, characters, places and inciden either are products of the author's imagination or used fictitiously. Any resemblance to actual persons, living or dead, events or locales, is purely and entirely coincidental

Printed in the USA
10 9 8 7 6 5 4 3 2 1

Also by David Taylor II:

My Alphabet is Colorful!

My Alphabet is Musical!

My Alphabet is My Pet!

Diary of a Chocolate Midas

Diary of a Smart Black Kid: Sixth Grade

Dear God: Why Doesn't Broccoli taste like Chocolate?

www.DavidTaylor2.net

Follow me on Twitter: @dt2author

Dedicated to
the superhero
in every child
and the super parents
that raise them!

My Alphabet is Super!
(Normies)

David Taylor II

HODT BOOKS, INC.

SKOKIE, IL

A is for Aquatic Powers

*You can breathe underwater

B is for Blaster Powers

*You can shoot power blasts from your hands and feet

C is for Chrono Powers

*You can freeze time

D is for
Duplication Powers

*You can make copies of yourself

E is for Elastic Powers

---

*You can stretch any part of your body out

F is for Flight Powers

*You can move through the air faster than a rocket

G is for Gravity Powers

*You can control gravity fields

H is for Healing Powers

*You can quickly heal any wound

I is for Invulnerability

*You can't be hurt by any attack

J is for Jinx Powers

*You can make others have bad luck

K is for
Kinetic Energy

*You can manipulate any energy that comes your way

L is for Light Beams

*You can shoot light energy from your chest

M is for Mirage Powers

---

*You can create mirages of yourself

N is for Negation Powers

*You can negate any power from anyone else

O is for

Optic Powers

---

*You have both telescopic vision and microscopic vision

P is for PyroKinetics

*You can shoot fireworks from your hand

Q is for Quartz Powers

---

*You have diamond hard skin

R is for

Runner Powers

---

*You can run
so fast you
light the ground
on fire

S is for Spiderweb Powers

*You can shoot your own spider's web

T is for Techno Shield

*You have a shield that can block any attack

U is for
Upside Down Powers

*You can flip anything upside down

V is for Velocity Powers

*You can change the speed of anything

W is for Warp Powers

*You can transport yourself through time and space in warp bubbles

X is for
X-Ray Powers

*You can make yourself see-through

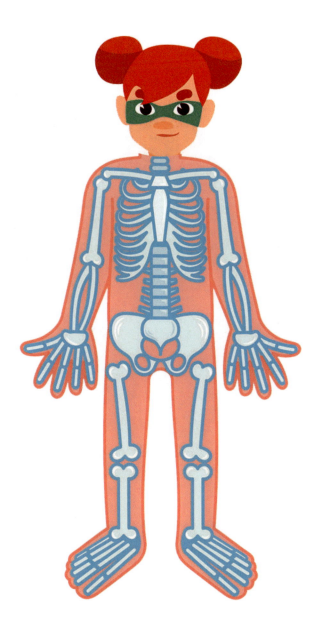

Y is for Yelling Powers

*You can magnify your voice louder than any other sound

Z is for Zephyr Powers

*You can float on, ride on, and control gentle winds

David Taylor II
loves to write books,
make music,
eat pizza,
and create superhero comics.
He was born in Evanston, IL.

www.DavidTaylor2.net

Follow on Twitter: @dt2author

Made in the USA
Middletown, DE
09 May 2019